Bled for Days

Dead for Months

Empyrean Grace

Content Warning

This poetry collection contains imagery and descriptions of domestic violence, rape, sexual assault, narcissistic maltreatment, suicidal ideation, and physical abuse.

Contents

Songs that Resonate with Each Poem

Rest without Sleep ("Atlas: Eight" by Sleeping At Last)

Bone Deep ("Bored" by Billie Eilish)

Beams of Light ("Cariño" by The Marías)

Holding You ("Cariño" by The Marías)

Dive in the Shallow Water ("Dissolve" by Absofacto)

The Red-Handed Culprit ("You Are the Coffin" by Flatsound)

Wide Open ("You Are the Coffin" by Flatsound

Rest without Sleep

Behind closed doors, pictures hiding
dents, my father shattering knuckles
against his daughter's face.
Anger transferred to pain
on a young, fragile frame.
The longing to understand how such torment
brings the sunrise into focus –
how such violence regards satisfaction to
my deceiver. Am I wrong to trust his words,
to hear something so empty and true, press
to reflect empty and true?
Did my eyes water when the breath escaped
from my lungs as his eyes covered my body
like a shadow?
How instantly the shadow becomes you.
You stole my last breath:
a pine drape on coffin, on casket.
There may have been people before you that
robbed me of my innocence,
that every slight touch turned to
many, but you –
you buried me six feet under.

Bone Deep

The aglet of laces and buttons on my jacket
milked your reflection.
A potential to warn and brace
the man before you came to me.

Tennis shoes glued to either foot,
a silent signal for an early leave.
Ditched by co-workers on game night,
the combination of solitaire and snowed-in roads.
A pile of ivory glided beyond apartments.
Solace and fresh glisten.

That thin smile –
I hadn't kissed a man before, but
fear dictated beyond comfort; it left little room for
choice.
The ceiling replaced by a looming height
and a 4 o'clock shadow.
His knees dug my shoulders into place,
the nape of my neck gripped with such force,
my head pulled forward.
Veiny fists and unforgiving push.
Pink, fuzzy handcuffs adorned disembodied
wrists.
That such a thing exists went over my head
as bruise after bruise grew on my left and right
thighs.
It means you're desirable –

the only compliment he spared.
Straitlaced lie condensed the window
with winter.
Lips were sealed; they weren't shut.
I could wash my
tongue,
throat,
and face,
but not the memory.

The former friend slapped my back pockets mid-
shift,
spitting unsavory names, undaunted eye contact.
HR refused to help,
department changes didn't change his ways,
and I couldn't erase
the parts of the man that killed me.
If he pointed a knife at my chest,
there would be nothing left to stab.
I quit the night shift.
My rumpled state
would soon belong to you.

Beams of Light

You're like sunshine.
I feel warm,
and loved,
and whole again.
His voice stung the air.
Cut through the slab above the couch.
A ravine in the thick heat of April.
The rain brought nothing but a bed of
dead roses.
My hands cupped the palms of puppy love.
His back to me before the sun rose
and the grass smelled of dew.
My nose nuzzled against the soft of his spine.
I looked for a departure, a surrender in his words,
so I could grab an excuse to ride my fear out of
discourse.
A candle wick dwindles.
I can't accept this fate,
but curiosity, stunned and still,
the shadow and the wick grew further
from who I was.
I hoped this moment would last
but not extend past the walls
of the remainder of my innocence.
Pity.

Holding You

Palm up and head turned.
My hand empty outstretched to you.
It was dark. I felt hidden and unnoticed,
even with windows down
and the moonlit trees a canopy of protection
from the strength I should have used
to run.
We took the backroads.
Your musk traveled to my heart.
It connected. It twisted.
The feeling *peace*
wringing my hands free of any warning.
He didn't want to say it,
but I did it anyway:
I love you.
I was first and remained as so.
These words I had said, those words you never
meant.
Warmth grounded me.
I looked at you and saw comfort.
I accepted the love I deserved.
Smiling gently as a passenger,
a dot in your rearview mirror.
I was further than I thought I was
to being close to you.

Dive in the Shallow Water

The first week, it felt off.
I was brittle, and then I cracked.
If I'm your object,
commodify my value with sedulous libido.
I've corroded undisciplined exposure.
Oxidized without will.
What more would it matter
if you took it a step further?

You were the large expanse:
a cloudy smog, the plastering blanket, blindfold
vision.
A field of heavy weeping.
I didn't want to spread my legs,
so you unbuttoned my struggles.
This isn't growth, and this isn't healing.
This conversation an endless pit,
where I kept the pulley and pail at the ready.
Every two weeks, it came up dry.
I was trapped and parched.
I wasn't myself.
Your every substance came to fruition, stood
steady as you are,
firmly stagnant.
Printed in the belief that you deserve every piece
of me.

So I shape-shifted and churned,

set sail and let go of the one thing I still had –
the last consent I had left to give –
I know God by His Peace,
but I knew you by your violence.
Shipwrecked with burning docks.
I wanted to dive head-first into cobblestone
before the moon drug the waves
to wash away rosebuds of tissue,
but your hold on my self-worth
made me rely on you for oxygen.

Second Base Comes First

You're taller,
you're stronger,
you're heavier --
when you lay on me like that.
I can't connect our mouths.
I can't count on my fingers
the number of times I said 'no.'
Your lips met mine.
I shivered.
I shuddered.
I broke.
Another part of me gone.
Another decision: taken.
Another first: disowned.
Your foot was in the door,
so tell me,
did I let you in?

The Red-Handed Culprit

I thought I had said 'no.'
Not once or twice, but more.
First, with my subtle expression,
then twice more with syllables.
Shaky words
slip off my tongue,
fell off the bed
and onto the floor,
unable to stand on their own.
A fourth with my tone.
A fifth with concern.
No.
I don't want this.
You ripped off my clothes,
the ones I held so tightly onto.
White knuckles from
battle and baton.
Trust was taken with linen shorts
and a black shirt.
A sixth 'no' was in the making
before guilt slipped in.
Why do you turn my 'no'
into a 'yes'?
Every part of who I am
denies you permission,
all except survival.
My 'yes' is not a 'yes';
If anything,
it's submission.
I want to blame guilt,

but all I can do is blame
myself.

Wide Open

The bed wasn't made.
It wasn't available.
It was a sign:
it was a refusal.
When my bed was made,
when it was available,
it was a sign:
it was a refusal.
Don't ask me to go deeper;
don't tell me when to swallow.

Embodiment of Shame

I'm not proud of you.
You creep in
without a knock,
without notice.
A whisper sprawled along
furrowed brows.
A push
and a shove.
You spit
and slash
at what lay before you.

The Blade Cuts the Cake

I wanted to see the care in your eyes,
but craving conquered hollowed sockets.
From a swivel chair to a once cozy corner,
not knowing what to feel,
inexperience withheld expectations.
Your knife unsheathed.
A threat to flesh.
A threat to love.
Reminding me of the pain –
of the bleeding down there.
A rudimentary feeling from elementary school.
The familiar fear of lights out and coffee breath:
a looming stature in the doorway
from a father figure and father alone.
I couldn't bear the memories that pain would
overwhelm,
but I had to please you.
If your knife couldn't split me in two,
it could at least pierce my tongue,
because your satisfaction
became my leash.

Personify Guilt

Are these thoughts my own?
From
the way
they puncture
my heart?
Twisting my tongue
and cheek.
Fighting tongue
and cheek,
for jurisdiction
over my actions.
That which wasn't there,
that was
before you came
along.

Backburner: I Will Stay

I thought I would enjoy who I would become
with you.
I thought you'd breathe a new life
in me,
but the smoke from your breath
stuck to these walls.
Labored breathing and good moments
few and far between.
Wound after wound piled in ways
I chose not to remember,
occurring often and often.
Dismembered.
Dislocated.
Your power lay in the shadows:
on this wrist and that ankle.
Comfort you didn't earn –
kindness you would take –
I allowed to give when I could afford it,
but you knew I was running
on empty.

You're Not Attractive

I was drawn to you,
no doubt,
but the underlying extrapolation
led me to the path mostly taken --
taken advantage of.
I was drawn to you,
no doubt,
but it took me a while to find you attractive.
Not that your fluffy dark curls laid low,
and your puppy dog eyes opened the floodgates
to everything alluring,
but that the syntax of your demeanor
covered my body like a still shadow.
When your words made me feel
of scrap and left a metallic taste:
an uncomfortable residue that made it hard
to believe you wanted to do
no harm.

You Know What You Want

The disproportionate,
the head over heels,
the now trending
thighs,
skin,
and bone.
Commercialize unequal esteem.
Do not be consumed by milky skin
and almond eyes.
Do not hold me with a gaze
hungry for my race,
by the short curve of my nose
and flatness of my face.
I am more than puffy under eyes,
sharp cheekbones, and
knock knees.
I am not your anime girl.
Don't say your fetish is my race.

False Truths

Marriage would give me security,
since certainty was either a quickened pace,
or for a long time to come.
Marriage then became
a covenant between God and two lovers.
A promise built on love,
not empty validation.
Without certified cognisance,
except there was one lover –
the other, a cloaked figure.
Attention unaffixed.
It wasn't acknowledged by the government,
but I wanted approval from God.
This is what I had to tell myself
so I could come to terms
that you took my
virginity.
Your gain was my loss.
I wasn't deflowered, no.
I was a lilac ripped from gravel.
I gave more and more of myself willingly,
but not driven by lust.
I wanted to hurt myself.
You're the only kind of attachment
I thought I was worth.
I was left penniless.
For an ounce for you to care,
was an ounce too much.
Every part of this crippled me.
If my pain was inconvenient for you,

why was I so convenient to have around?
You wanted me dead,
and you did just that.

That's Enough

Watching the paint dry,
it dragged me down.
I refuse to be happy
until I hear thunder
from the front steps
and an alert from our camera.

Hey, love.
I'll play it cool.
To you, who means the world to me
and melts my heart,
let me carry your backpack, worries and all.
The patchwork of softness
spread from my face to yours.
Your voice lifts my spirits,
smelling sweetly of mowed grass, cologne, a
breath of fresh air.
I see happiness, beams of light, the dust dancing
in gentle sun.
The doormat and coat rack.
The cook and the nurse.
Please lean on me.
I want to be needed.

Nailed from undercurrent to instability
made me refuse the truth.
Everything is plastic,
from your smile

and my response,
to the tension
and the silence.

I won't ever be enough
if you seek comfort in me.
I won't ever be enough
if I seek comfort in you.

Let me eat my words.
Emboldened in self-sabotage on an empty plate
and an empty stomach.
This uneven staccato
is why I stay alert and awake.

The rise and fall of torso
remains ever so
imbalanced.
It's in retrospect that I realized
my heart refused to beat
until you.

Be My Shelter

I entered your chest
in a crestfallen slumber.
I learned how to count pulses,
to hear arrhythmia after arrhythmia.
The S1 and S2 at APETM.
We met at Erb's point.
I was taught about how the body compensates
and bilateral equality,
but what I felt was my heart
ceasing,
tumbling,
and forgetting what blood was.
A hypertrophy turned sour.
The knife in my chest and the knife in my back.
In this warm crevice I created by your side,
your reluctant hold on my arm,
my ear and the apical cadence.
I learned to care for people,
while my body compensated
functioning with the absence of love
in the warmth of your chest.

He Who is Living in the World

You are not above all things.
You are not my savior.
You are not my world.
I don't trust you.
With knife and fork, stake my heart.
Eat my honor.
Eat my grace.
He is my God;
you are not God.
Being isolated by choice in your head: an echo
chamber.
The ricocheted, crystal clear, fun house of a
home,
don't probe for information
to disagree on disbelief.
Please ask for answers,
not for open wounds.

Obsession Rotting Away

Did I tell you how much you mean to me?
My mind framed portraits
of interlaced fingers.
Conduction of heat, one palm to the next.
Did I tell you that it's my fault?
Because you've given me more than enough
signs.

I am without worth
with you.

It was written to be read.
All these novels on the shelves of our basement,
I pass it day by day,
and dwell on it behind stars.
You never meant to craft such
luminescence for me,
regarding the ship you sailed
before you even boarded.
Prohibited to speak it into existence:
All my likes and dislikes,
way of thinking,
and time spent
were unimportant to you.
I can make your nose crinkle
and laughter thunder from the inside,
while my heart lay limp before you buried me.
Every shovel of dirt

hit like stone.
Marinate in denial,
cut into my flesh,
because nothing could hurt more
than your empty words of endearment.

Alarm Bells Go Silent

Steam leaked under the door.
Meander forward,
fog and foe,
into the gutter,
that which your mind takes form.
Humid to the touch,
fear to the taste.
Pressed against fresh memories.

Vision swimming from
a hot shower and heavy mind.
Don't blame my nakedness on your nature.
Don't corner me:
A fish out of water.

Breath blistered down my neck,
an outline traced by fingertip.
You said you wanted to be selfish
just this once.
You said you wanted me
to pretend I'm not scared.
Locked jaw.
Pale in the face.
I couldn't look up and couldn't kiss back.
Veins stuttered from the unnatural heat
of the corpse in front of me.
My mouth, the image of sullen disembark,
penumbra of gloom.

What an endearing promise.
How sincere.
How genuine.
Just this once,
I'll part my lips
to say and to do,
speak sweetly of sugar,
act out of yielding,
and you'll treat me worse than foul play.
I'll give you everything
just to watch you shove it down my throat.
I'll be a shell of myself
for your content.
Shame, humiliation, guilt, and praise;
my chagrin of respect cemented your ignorance.

Here Love Lies

I'm scared to start something
that will break me,
tie me up,
breathe me in,
leave me breathless
in your embrace.
I cannot walk;
I cannot breathe.
You're my everything.
I want this,
and that scares me.

Rosy ears
bled to my heart.
My fingertips yearn
to know
where your smile
starts and ends.
I'm up in the hilltops,
but knee-deep in your love.
Your warmth
is everything
that makes me
weak.

I saw you in pink.
Sunbeams flickered
among the forest awning.

I followed your steps,
I looked for your hand,
while you looked
ahead.
The undergrowth
grabbed at my feet.
I was left alone
waiting.

I vacillate,
balancing back and forth,
through and through,
down a staircase.
This spiral
feels empty.
I want nothing more
than to reach the end.

Don't run your fingers through my hair.
Don't tell me I'm pretty.
Don't hold my hand.
Please --
just love me back.

Please Don't Go

Comfort me.
Dig the knife and dip it forward.
Use me,
because I can't calm down.
My lungs won't move.
When I think of the reality of the situation,
use me.
I need a distraction;
I can't feel anything.
After you had your way with me,
stay like this,
because this is the only way
I could get you to hug me
and hold my hands,
even if they're pinned above my head
in a bruising force.
No indication of
deep-seated concern
or a glimmer of safekeeping
in those eyes.
Please stay like this.
I need your warmth right now.
I need your weight on me.
Don't go.
Eat me whole,
break my heart,
crush me,
cave me in,
then leave me for dead.

Soul Deep Scars Remain an Entrance for Sunlight

A zipper that unzips.
The skin sets the pace.
The body takes notes,
tracing fiber tracing marrow.
Forearm to wrist.
Skin to skin.
Set the pace.
Trading pain for pain;
bargaining sacrifice for suffering.
This self-inflicted sorrow
feels alive and awake.
Fury unearthed the rolling, the rumbling of crash.
A whisper only peace can hear.
Stained crimson with a hot breath.
Let it welcome what it wants;
let it welcome love and grace.

Sword of Damocles

A known sexual predator:
your cousin, twice my age,
locked eyes with his prey.
Shuttered windows for eyes,
litter,
and chipped paint,
begged for a new coat.
Hiding coins with
the constant slapping of wristwatch
on bar stools.
The topography of stolen stories
from ringlet after ringlet on a 2,000-dollar chain.

With dreamlike slowness,
his cup tiptoed on uneven lips.
The washboard, rugged trails poured mist.
My waterline now a blindsided brazen.
Hearkened to you, my love.
I'll wait for your guide and arm, a diversion from
this path –
ardent gasp, concentrate
on the fallen matador.
He didn't aim at my grief, but beyond it.
A frenetic game
doused in gasoline.
The egregious act in regal bearing
bore teeth.
Yet, you smiled.

She needs this for her healing.

What does that even mean?
If I'm touched by another father,
it'll heal me of my own?
If I step foot in the neighborhood
tasting such bitter things:
the color of
spoiled bleach and
rotting milk,
it'll erase the trevail?
If I unclothe deep regret and
mirthful company,
your needle will puncture holes only to slacken
the thread.
I shouldn't have to tell you my background
to feel heard.
I shouldn't have to tell you the hurt
to be taken seriously.
You're built for violence.
Sword of Damocles,
you may be above me,
but not in the way you think.

Panic Attack

Highway hypnosis a few moments
from the house.
It's happening again.
I cannot pinpoint a specific cause, but sensations
flounder and flail.
I hate this feeling.
I am filth,
I am bone,
but I am human.
Tear me out of my own skin.
This is too much.
Thoughts won't shut off.
At the fifth intercostal space,
center left, beneath the sternum
is the pounding and cacophony
of a nauseating blow.
My mind tells me I'm dying
in clouded focus
unfazed.
On hind legs,
fold inward in pitch-black descent.

He appeared squatting,
square shoulder next to me.
A soft touch.
Forbearing de novo.
The connection between palm and shoulder
enkindled down to Earth.
The seconds sludged in thick reform.
He was so kind

and so gentle.
I hold onto this briefness,
because he handed me empathy
on a silver platter.

Rekindle my Strength

This time,
I won't let you hold me down against my bed
against my will.

This time,
I won't let you block the door,
push me,
and shake my shoulders hard
at the mention of throbbing burn marks
gained from falling in love,
until I forget that I asked to break up –
forget that you ever made me feel safe.
I won't let your power
hinder my own,
and drive me back to you
with less freedom than the last.

This time,
I won't let you scream my name
so loud I freeze and hold my breath.
I lay still
as you take what you've taken,
night after night.
The forced Spanglish lodged in your throat;
such soft words don't suit you.
A disguise behind doe eyes
and pouting lips.

This time,
I'll try hard not to be so easily convinced

to not tell my sister and your brother
what you told me not to tell,
the things that you did:
The way you skinned me from the inside out.

Tear Drops Kiss the Skin

I love you,
he said.
You're beautiful and nice to me.
These words were drawn out,
an intricate mirage of tapestry
tied up in scarlet enhance.
He drew out these words,
pushed them through the printing press
for articles of satire,
instruments of fun.

I felt so worn,
a faded afterthought of who I used to be.
I let him in,
and it broke me,
so I broke up with him.

The click of basement door
and slick slam of rollers on wood.
It grew silent.
I never loved you,
he said.
You're hot when you cry,
he moaned and grabbed and pushed away any
attestation.
Echoes of the past rang louder than the evening
halo.
Prior screams of separation and despair.
My words couldn't shoulder the weight.
You're so convenient –

This admittance
wasn't a stab in the heart;
it was the hand that took my own,
cut it deep into my veins.
I don't care anymore.
Pour salt,
take shards of glass,
and scatter them on the floor.
Push the soles of my feet on
floorboard over floorboard.

Like the scars on my wrist
and the cards we were dealt,
I still find you in places.
You're everywhere I turn,
everywhere but
when I need you.

A Nail in the Coffin

My ears are ringing.
The volume,
the waves,
rise with the sound
of love songs
I associated with your smile.
My heart impaled
by vocal cords
overused,
overturned.
I don't know if it was
fear or love.
It's so loud.
Damper the noise,
damper the humming;
let my heart collapse
in dead silence.

Prayer for the Born Again

Dear Lord,
Forgive me for turning a blind eye,
I spoke of You in glowing terms
and threw pearls in the pig pen. My walls torn
down,
a renovation two steps backward on opposite
trails.
I stopped feeling worthy in thicket dethroned.
Forgive me for decisions disguised as willingness,
grievances, hid under Your wing. I didn't fall
from grace
but landed in Your lap.
The Lord cradled me in a way I couldn't
comprehend.
Even now, with eyes closed,
there's no difference knowing whether he is there
or not –
whether the lights are on or off.
It doesn't matter
if I'm still scared of him.
Please grant me understanding and patience to
see:
How did I not know the Shepherd is with us,
even when the sheep are blind?

14:00

Dosage calculations.
Numbers by the spoonful.
The dining table a platform for markers
and dotted paper.
Come here, he challenged.
We're broken up, I answered.
Pencil shook,
finger paused on conversions of IVs with
weight-based drugs.
Intramuscular injections
and tall man lettering.
I clutched the turtleneck,
hiding bite marks
spread eagle lilac.
Excuses in assessment lab
when stethoscope hits the skin,
lung sounds spoke volumes
next to marks left by him.
Give me a kiss,
Please trust,
I'll feel better,
I'll feel good.
These moments confirmed
the downfall of sharing a roof and not a home.
My boundaries were made of mortar and of clay.
The pit of those words
were bricks tied to my legs.

You're a Therapist

Si, si, si
You said,
when you're told you're considerate,
while you're hurting others.
When you're told you're the prodigy,
but your mind, an iron fist.
When you're told you're like Jesus,
but you are furthest from Christ-like.
I can't fathom independence:
the false belief that you can be a comforter
for family members you've
stolen and robbed livelihood,
money, security, or happiness.
I cannot celebrate the likeness
of someone who denies empathy.
It's not enough.
Go on and tread forth,
create flashbulb memories
that line up on different timelines
or frequencies.
Go on and ruin marriages,
house savings,
or parent-child relationships.
Wreck my belongings while you're high on
drugs:
my car for your happiness, twenty minutes, two
towns over.
Smoke marijuana and drive a prostitute
downtown
on my 22nd birthday.

Look straight through me unless you're horny or
hungry.
Go on and scorch everyone in your path,
because your palms are layered with
bloodshed from loved ones
you never loved.
Only you can clean your hands,
but your thirst can't be quenched from a kitchen
sink.

The Notebook

Door frame demented.
Your thoughts far worse than unhinged.
Bloodshot fervor.
Half a notepad and a pen.
A confession reached my flesh and blood.
You said it with tears,
you said the truth:
you said that you took advantage of me
to my oldest sister;
you said that you couldn't save me
from yourself.
The hallway dimly lit
honesty in a plaster of
heaving sobs.
The sharp sting of tongue and brisk air
paled in comparison to
pseudo-sincerity.

Put it on paper.
Write it word for word.
Goodness after goodness reaches your plate.
Iniquity turned to lust.
But why are my knees bruised
and arms bleeding,
while you're unyielding without
worry?
The strings you've attached –
the values you propose –
are prices tagged to our heads.
You took back your apology,

but not the damage you've done.

The Lone Wolf is not the Omega

Red, white, and blue flashed by your window.
A patrol stationed neighborly in fashion,
unknowing upon arrival.
Searching for a lost dog,
addressing a break-in, or
perhaps a deliverance of the subpoena
to the man down the road.

Red, white, and blue sped away,
yet picked up your heart rate.
The officer didn't step forward
nor indicate you on his radar.

Red, white,
it's untrue that you raped me,
from the eyes of a rapist –
from the likes of you.
So why were you worried
in close proximity to an officer?
Why did you assume
I reported you for acts of violence
you so strongly deny?
Why did you run to your mother
to say that I made you rape me
and grab my chest?
I am without personality;
an absentminded exterior;
a sex addict;
I'm the girl with the brain size of a pea and
manipulative agenda page after page.

Even five months post-breakup,
your truth alone
caught like wildfire.
A tidal wave could not subdue
the depths at which your family
would not let me hear the end of it.
Until I wanted to end it.
My life, that is.

Mama's Boy

He's got a lock of thick hair,
an adventurous twenty-something:
He's your kiddo.
He's got drive, gut, and grit:
He's your kiddo.
He's the kind of guy that pursues virgins and
misfits.
The kind of guy
who sits and stares,
stuck on daydreams of conspiracy theories
and matters of *his* mind.
The kind of guy who creates a stampede
to trample shouts and bellows.
A bungalow of stew-roasted opinions.
A bigot and misogynist.
And you'll stand by him:
a motionless supporter,
a proud mother of a son who is
a taker, not a giver.
He's back at home
with a gaming setup and dumbbells,
being served by the spoonful,
charging others by the dime.
He's upbeat with a great taste in music:
He's your kiddo.
Native to a different State and a lover of travel:
He's your kiddo.
A rapist, an abuser:
He's your kiddo.
But a monster? No;

he's the son of one.

The Words I Kept to Myself

To the flowerbed of thorns,

I deeply apologize for the inconvenience of having burdened your family; however, my intention was not to cause harm to those in which it did. Feelings are entitled to the owner. Thus, I am sincerely sorry for the aches and pains that have laid heavy on your heart. I left work in the middle of my shift to clear the air of your worries.

As I sit here at your dining table looked down upon as a slut, I will look up to each and every face and know I am not beneath you. I want him to heal so he does not hurt himself or others. I, too, want to heal. Thank you for being so kind as to speak Spanish to me when you're eager to use inappropriate words that hit below the belt. It may be a language I don't understand, but I can tell that you mean well when you make my misfortune about yourself.

YES, YOUR ADULT SON IS NOT A RAPIST BECAUSE HE WAS NOT A STRANGER IN THE DARK ALLEY.

YES, IT MAKES PERFECT SENSE THAT WHEN I WAS RAPED, I WAS NOT A VICTIM BECAUSE I DIDN'T KICK AND SCREAM.

YES, ALTHOUGH I EXPLICITLY DID NOT WANT TO LOSE MY VIRGINITY, IT WAS HE WHO WAS MANIPULATED INTO HAVING SEX WITH ME.

YES, I CAME BACK TO HIM BECAUSE I WANTED HIM TO CARE FOR ME KNOWING THAT HE WOULD RAPE ME THE SAME NIGHT I WAS ASSAULTED BY A CO-WORKER.

YES, I AM PROJECTING WHAT MY FATHER DID TO ME ONTO YOUR SON SINCE HIS ACTIONS ARE NOT HIS OWN.

YES, I THINK THAT IT IS BY NO MEANS DISRESPECTFUL TO YOU AND YOUR EX-HUSBAND TO SUPPORT THE RAPIST YOU CALL YOUR CHILD.

YES, HE HAD INSTILLED BATTERY, ASSAULT, AND DOMESTIC VIOLENCE, BUT TO YOU, MY SUBMISSION WAS WHAT MADE HIM HURT ME.

YES, IT'S MY FAULT; YES, YOU ARE THE ONLY ONES IN PAIN.

YES, I SHOULD APOLOGIZE TO YOU.

YES, SIR. YES, MA'AM.

Your son ended up just like you, charisma and all. You raised him well.

Bled for Days Dead for Months

Goodnight;
It was anything but.
The mattress dipped by my side,
a palm bloomed in a manner --
a repulsion from my hip.
This warmth ricocheted iterations:
ten years with my father,
relentless adolescence from an uncle,
two co-workers,
and a thirty-year-old.
I'm dirty.

I'm dirty. I'm dirty. I'm dirty.

With them and with him,
my body was given a choice:
fight or flight,
and yet it always chose to freeze.
my voice with shallow exhale respite
buried beneath the dense partition
of sundered lamentations,
added weight to these shoulders,
and a noose to my neck.
I was pushed,
pulled,
and bitten.
Squeezed shut.
I drew back.
Left with redness and blues:
Neck, chest, hinge of upper thigh.

The apex and the knife.
Teeth sunken in further;
this deepness isn't love.
It's a weapon; I'm a martyr.
The aridity hushed.
Surroundings a deafening defeat.
I caved in the stillness.
Bled for days.
Dead for months.
The minute hand an abiding reminder of your
touch,
stapled steady to what was left of my essence.
I didn't give myself permission to heal,
but I didn't give you permission
to break me.

Please hear the seams rip;
tear apart what was already battered.
Show me where it hurts.
I want to know how to reach your heart –
not substantiate the truth;
not warrant my collapse,
but to find reason for reasoning,
to heal the seed and guide the roots.

Pinion the outer banks,
dove-like in appendage.
A softhearted flutter ceased from pluck, uproot,
and heave.
Sweet temperance hold me close, placing hand
over heart.
Encircle the debris plume crest on the landing.
Flightless with you; earthbound unvarying.
These wings are clipped.

Moxie backbone serenity.
While legs bear the weight,
Lord, bear my cross.
Carry me.
Two prints in the sand –
bring me to pieces and toughen these bones.
Ball and socket; tender turn.
I cannot fly, but I can run.
I am more than lost innocence.
Clean hands unacquainted and
clipped wings on the floor.
My cage firm in your hold when ball and shackle
break.
Vindication gave reverence
from the residual forgiveness
meant for you.
Meant for me.
My white flag endearment:
A confident surrender.
An old bruise grew no further
than the soles of my feet.
flightless bird that can bound –
I'll soar with these legs –
and fly without wings.

The following piece is the first poem I wrote in 2019. I was a teenager. Coming from a low-income household, we couldn't afford to uproot our lives if my father found out where we lived after my parents divorced eight years prior. He had stalked us before, but it ended within a matter of months.

Unfortunately, he managed to discover which high school I attended and warned that he would see me at graduation. Forgiveness doesn't equal earned trust. It was at this point I so badly wanted to die because he could end up hurting the people I held close to my heart: my family.

To Him

Dear dad,

I forgive you
for not knowing what love is,
for making my mom think she found love in you.
For not knowing who Christ is,
and if you found Him before us,
I wouldn't have to forgive you.

I forgive you
for convincing me manipulation was marriage,
for pushing my pregnant mother out of the car,
for wanting to abort my older sister,
for leaving your fruit and bearer,
in isolation on an island.
As you never wanted to lay down your sins,
as you lay in your filth with other women.

I forgive you
for making all of us hold in our screams,
for leaving my arms with leopard print.
A hollowed-out barrel.
Tarnished rings.

I forgive you
for making me a people pleaser, because
the only way I could end up alive was if I
pleased you.

I forgive you

for throwing me in the garage --
just how you threw your third wife in the
dumpster.
Her first step in America;
my first time finding your pornography.

I forgive you
for permitting me not to say no.
Even when I want to,
even if I can't breathe,
even if my grip has gone
rusted red like the Lion
you vowed to serve next to
The Torch,
for melting your feelings
and branding my heart –
to think love was interchangeable with fear.

I forgive you
for making us countdown the days
to see if we would make it to our teens,
because your beatings were becoming worse,
but our will to live was growing deeper.
Deeper than the cuts you carved on our skin
and in our hearts;
louder than the click of the camera,
the shutter that shivered down my spine as your
young daughters
lay lifeless on the couch without clothes
in positions we didn't understand.

I forgive you
for making me blame myself every day,
for making me hate every inch about me,

for making me hate every thought I think,
for controlling me
when you're no longer there.

I forgive you
for thinking I'm not your daughter,
because I will still call you Dad,
because my cheekbones scream it for me;
my bone structure spells it out.
I will cling to the memories of when you were a
glimpse of a father:
the early mornings at Camel's Back,
the late nights at Country Donuts,
and the times when your stories were just stories.
I will remember him,
and I will remember you.
I choose to recognize all of who you are:
a heartbeat that once sounded
like my own.

I forgive *you*,
and yet I haven't forgiven *myself*.
I still love *you*,
and yet I don't know how to love *myself*.

蛋糕wavy

About the Author

I am a first-time author writing under the pen name, 'Empyrean Grace.' This pseudonym encompasses the ethereal aspects of poetry, as it carries a heartfelt nod to my deep connection with my faith in God. My decision to remain anonymous is rooted in the desire to protect my family's privacy and the personal stories I explore within my work.

My poetry is grounded in emotions, often created during moments of intrapersonal vulnerability. When pen hits paper, it becomes an outlet to heal wounds of the heart. I hope my poetry resonates with you, offering consolation and comfort when needed.

Connect with me at Empyrean Grace on Goodreads, @gracempyrean on Instagram, and gracempyrean@gmail.com for business inquiries.

Acknowledgements

While poetry and painting are vehicles necessary for processing pain, my deep gratitude to those who are standing pillars in my life underscore the gravity upheld in art form.

Bryan: In the prominence of hardship between deadlifts and cleans, you've helped me with knee injuries and mental obstacles I would otherwise have ignored. As a reflection of God's love and light, you've allowed so many people to come to Christ with how you hold yourself. Your comfort stretched beyond the gym floor, offering the kind of nurture I longed for from a father figure.

Ayako: A special place in my heart is carved just for you. The gentle nature of your unwavering kindness is a constant reminder of how non-linear healing is. You are painted inside out as a caring support system, and behind your profession, roles, and titles is a wonderful, sincere person. You taught me that I cannot eliminate trauma solely because it is painful, but I can make choices in places I thought there were none.

Mrs. Atkins: After the commencement of my high school graduation, I remember sitting with you in your empty classroom. I was excited to have you sign my yearbook in peace since a flood of students vied for your signature days prior. Before embarking on the nursing program, you enlightened me with the realization that our calling does not always align with our initial ambitions. I now know that you saw something in me that I myself was afraid to unveil. Thank you for planting a seed of encouragement I hold onto to this day.

Dr. Llewellyn: Strong-willed and heartfelt, your authenticity in healthcare is more than an uplifting remembrance; I'm certain that everyone who encounters you is imprinted with deep appreciation. You listen when it matters. You care when it matters. You make no excuses. Thank you for being an example of what true resilience and raw compassion look like.

David Luiz: Your steadfast guidance as a Project Manager goes beyond the distinctive client-leader relationship. Your existence is a gift in itself; the word "grateful" does not even scratch the surface of my respect to encompass your dedication and overall demeanor.

Amazon Publishing Writing Team: Boundless thanks to my devoted writing team for their invaluable attention to detail. The prowess necessary to format this book truly encapsulated the essence of these poems.

Amazon Publishing Design Team: Much appreciation goes out to my design team for their meticulous eye and skillful commitment, preserving the personal touches that brought my hand-painted cover to its full potential.